PUERTO RICO TRAVEL GUIDE

A SMART VACATION PLANNER WITH FACTS, TIPS, AND THINGS TO DO FOR LE$$ THAN YOU'D BELIEVE.

Happy Holidays Guides

DEDICATION

To all our social media friends, for their support.

"One's destination is never a place,
but a new way of seeing things."

~Henry Miller

CONTENTS

.

ACKNOWLEDGMENTS

We would like to acknowledge the efforts of every individual and organization who have contributed to the rebuilding, restoration, and revitalization of Puerto Rico in the wake of Hurricane Maria.

The tropical beauty of the island is self-evident, but the strength and solidarity of the Puerto Rican community is just as inspiring.

1. AN EXOTIC ISLAND GETAWAY WITHIN REACH

Scenic Potala Pastillo beach in Ponce, PR.

When you think of clear blue waters, palm trees and rainforests, does that seem like an impossible dream to you?

What if we told you that we scored an unbelievable vacation package and had an unforgettable tropical island getaway for less than four figures each? And that includes flight, hotel, food, everything!

On our last day in Puerto Rico, we were so astonished at how much we had packed into five days – on a budget, no less! – that we decided right then and there to write a book and share it with the world. "This is too good to be true," we thought.

We agreed that with a little planning and following the same tips and tricks we employed, anyone can do this. We started writing down notes for this book on the airplane ride back. No kidding.

The tips we're sharing within will likely save you hundreds of dollars. And whether you are on a budget or not, we want to share with you the amazing experiences you can have in Puerto Rico – memories of a lifetime.

Why should you consider visiting Puerto Rico?

- Ranked as the top spring break family travel destination by Family Travel Magazine in 2013.
- Year-round temperatures average 70° in the mountains and 80° at sea level in this tropical marine climate.
- Beaches of every variety (light to dark sand) in every direction.
- One of the most popular cruise ports in the Caribbean.
- If you live in the U.S., the U.S. dollar is the official currency, you do not need a passport, and electrical outlets (110V) do not require adapters.

The island is so beautiful, and offers such distinct experiences between the mountains and the beaches that we have included notes on exploring both. By the time you're done reading this book, you should have clear ideas on:

- An overview sketch of the island, including landscape, music and food
- Where and when to look for amazing travel deals
- Specific money-saving strategies worth hundred$
- Where to go online for booking, supplies, and supplemental info (over 50 links!)
- Whether or not you should rent a car
- The types of attractions you are most interested in
- How to fit those activities into your vacation itinerary
- Costly mistakes to avoid (learn from our experience!)

We were intent on getting a taste of what the *real* Puerto Rico had to offer – not just the sanitized-for-your-protection resorts. And the intention isn't to micro-manage where you eat or what you do. The intention is to offer up some of the best of what Puerto Rico has to offer so you can make your own decisions on what your must-see destinations might be. What does that mean, exactly? Well...

Are you willing to wander out beyond your hotel? Good!

Are you the type of person who knows that excitement and magic lie just outside your comfort zone? Excellent!

Before we begin, we'd like to share a note about the photos in this book:

WE TOOK EVERY SINGLE ONE OF THEM.

You won't see them anywhere else – 100% guaranteed. For those of you with a black and white reader, never fear – we have included links to some online full color photo essays so you can get to know the island better.

Additionally, we'd like to share a question that has been a key motivator after initially publishing this book:

WHAT CAN WE OFFER OUR READERS BEYOND THE BOOK?

And then the answer came clear as day: more information that we can't include in an e-book! As convenient as a digital book is, it can't offer you video or sound or a huge volume of photos. So we arrived at a solution to create an online resource portal whose link and overview we'll share in Chapter 8.

And now, off to the enchanted island we go...

2. GETTING TO KNOW PUERTO RICO

Puerto Rico (literally "rich port" in Spanish) is a beautiful Caribbean island offering diverse culture, beautiful geography, delicious cuisine, soulful music, and friendly people. You'll see many of the local license plates printed with "Isla del Encanto," which means "Island of Enchantment."

We're going to be honest – we've both been to three different Hawaiian islands, and when we were considering the amount of time and money it would take to get back there, we started investigating other options. And the more we looked at Puerto Rico, the more we saw it as something we wanted to explore.

And ultimately after visiting, we found ourselves asking, "Why isn't this more popular?" Especially if you don't live on the west coast of the U.S., it is absolutely more economical and accessible while offering landscapes to rival that of Hawaii.

Especially if you are willing to venture out beyond the resort (you are, aren't you?) the rewards are immense. But on to our overview...

Big, heavy books have been written about each of the following topics – our intention is to give you a short briefing only. However, we encourage you to learn more about this fascinating island before and after your visit.

A Brief Island Overview

Two-minute history: Puerto Rico was inhabited by the Taíno Amerindians until Christopher Columbus claimed the island for Spain in 1493. It was under Spanish rule until it was ceded to the U.S. according to the Treaty of Paris in 1898. Since that time, it has remained an unincorporated territory of the U.S. (as a commonwealth), with some inhabitants favoring the status quo, some interested in statehood, and some pushing for complete independence. Though many people speak English, Spanish is the dominant language so you may want to brush up (key driving terms listed in Chapter 5, language pointers Chapter 14).

The People: The 3.6 million islanders are predominantly European (75%), with the remaining 25% comprised of Native, African, Asian and mixed ethnicities. In our experience, the people were overwhelmingly friendly and warm – using terms of endearment with strangers is the norm. We got a sense of island pride that may come from the solidarity emerging from the many political and cultural transitions the islanders have experienced.

The Scenery: Covering over five thousand square miles, the island's geography, topology and climate are surprisingly diverse. From the warm, flat, windy beaches to the cooler, humid mountains (up to 4,000 feet high!) there is a lot to appreciate on this island. Oh, and we hope you like green, because almost everywhere you look you'll find large, lush tropical foliage.

The Food: Walking into any restaurant is a delight for the senses, with spices and seasonings which are savory, spicy, and very aromatic. The influences are a blend of native Indian (the Taíno), Spanish influence and Caribbean cross-pollination (Cuba, Haiti, etc). Read more detail in Chapter 6.

The Music: We dare you not to fall in love with the soulful tunes of Puerto Rico, from the sexy salsa to the heavy beats of reggaeton and the infectious merengue. You don't have to be an expert to appreciate this music – in fact we recommend that you tune to local stations both in your hotel and in your rental car to experience the full range of styles. We promise it will be the perfect soundtrack to your stay.

Did You Know? Interesting Island Facts

- The Taíno indian name for the island is Boriken or Borinquen, so you will often see things classified as "Boricua" or "Borinqueño" (Puerto Rican)

- The world's largest rum distillery is claimed by Bacardí and is located in Old San Juan. (Curiously, Bacardí originated in Cuba but moved to Puerto Rico in 1909.)

- The world's largest astronomical single-dish radio telescope is located in the Arecibo Observatory and has been collecting data for the SETI (Search for Extra-Terrestrial Intelligence) Project since 1999.

- El Yunque is the only tropical rainforest in the US National Park System.

- If you have the time, you can potentially enjoy over 270 miles of Puerto Rican beaches.

- San Juan is the second-oldest city in the Americas (founded in 1521), second only to the Dominican Republic's city of Santo Domingo.

- The piña colada was invented in Old San Juan.

- The islands of Vieques and Culebra are nesting grounds for endangered leatherback turtles.

- From 1892 to 1954 the U.S. made it illegal to display the Puerto Rican flag (sad but true).

- Popular Christmas song "Feliz Navidad" was written by Puerto Rican José Feliciano.

- The Cathedral of San Juan is one of the oldest in the Western Hemisphere, built in the 1520s.

For Reference: Visitor Center Information

Puerto Rico Tourism Company – Main Office
La Princesa Bldg. #2 Paseo La Princesa
Old San Juan, P.R. 00902
Telephone: 787-721-2400

3. AIRFARE – HOW TO SAVE REAL (POSSIBLY BIG) MONEY

View from the plane: watch for turquoise waters below.

Airfare

Generally speaking, your two biggest vacation expenses will be airfare and lodging. As you may know, airfare can vary wildly – each passenger on a commercial flight likely paid a different price for their ticket depending on timing, demand, and availability.

The good news is that you may be able to reduce your expenses if you're willing to do a little research up front. Remember that as consumers we generally pay for convenience, so if you're not in a hurry you could enjoy a significant discount on airfare. Here are five things to consider when scouting for the best flight deals:

Are you willing to drive to a hub or nearby airport? Do you have a relative or friend you can visit who lives in a city with an airport hub? Say you live in Tucson, AZ. If you're willing to drive to Phoenix you may find a lower fare *and* have one less layover. It also pays to search the other way: many travel sites allow you to search nearby airports when the hub airport flights may be full (more expensive).

Experiment with different departure and arrival days. Travel search engines often offer you different times, but sometimes just leaving one day before or after will save you money. Some of the airfare search engines allow you to check a box for "flexible dates" so make sure to select this option. Generally, a rule of thumb is to stay over at least one Saturday.

Consider combining fares. We're so accustomed to buying tickets round-trip through one airline, but sometimes it's worth checking two separate one-way fares – remember, you will pay less for flights that are trying to fill up their seats, so this is worth a shot.

Take the time to comparison shop. Check the same flight on all the big travel sites (Expedia, Travelocity, Orbitz, Kayak), and also on the individual airlines. Just a few minutes could save you enough to stay an extra day!

Don't forget to check your miles. If you have miles or points with the airline offering the best deal, make sure to check and see if you can offset some or all of the cost.

Explore vacation package deals. Often, hotels will team up with airlines for mutual benefit, often to boost travel and tourism during the "off season." (More on this in Chapter 4.) This means there are some deep discounts for combining airfare/lodging/car rental.

Air and Lodging Package Secret Weapon

For Puerto Rico, our go-to source for an airfare/lodging package was CheapCaribbean.com. We are happy to recommend them based on the fantastic combined discount, an outstanding personal experience and the great pre- and post-trip communication. Although flight and hotel rates vary by the minute, here is a real test case we completed side-by-side:

> *Airfare:* Atlanta, GA to San Juan Intl Airport, for a 5-night stay in October by airline carrier Spirit Airlines.
>
> *Lodging:* The Wyndham Grand in Rio Grande, PR (near the Rainforest).
>
> *Booked separately through airline and hotel websites:* $310 airfare + 1,129.71 hotel = $1,439 per person.
>
> *Booked through Cheap Caribbean:* $640 per person for the same exact flights and same room type. Both figures include final taxes and fees. That is a startling difference of over 50% savings!

Other Travel Resources

You likely already have a list of travel sites bookmarked on your browser, but it won't hurt to look at this list and double-check for new ones to add to your tool chest.

Start with the big travel sites. Always check these when doing fare searches in case one has a discount over the same flights. Note that many of these now have mobile apps available for your price-comparison convenience! Here you'll find airfare, lodging, car rentals, vacation packages, and cruises.

Expedia.com. Expedia began as a Microsoft company and was later spun off as its own organization. It has established itself as a major player in the travel world, with localized web sites for 29 countries.

Priceline.com. Priceline, possibly most recognized for its famous spokesman William Shatner, is popular among travelers because it offers a way to search last-minute deals and allows you to bid your price for hotels, airfare and car rental. This works well especially if your travel dates and lodging are somewhat flexible. However, you may not know which organization will meet your winning bid, so there is a little uncertainty but savings can be big – they claim up to 60%, and that might be worth it.

Kayak.com. This site is a rising star, with cofounders from Expedia, Travelocity and Orbitz joining forces in 2004 with a vision of providing a better user experience. Kayak has localized web sites in 27 countries and allows you to compare many different air/lodging/car providers in an easy interface.

Travelocity.com. Travelocity was begun in 1996 as a subsidiary of SABRE holdings – the organization that to date was only available to airlines and travel agents. All the basic air/lodging/car/cruise/package booking and also offers international deals.

Orbitz.com. Founded in 1999 by a group of U.S. airlines, it was later acquired, merged with additional online travel companies and is now publicly traded. It is similar to the above online sites in terms of comprehensive offerings.

Sign up for deal alerts. You can create a folder in your e-mail program and funnel all travel communications there so you can read them at your leisure. Here are two favorites:

Airfarewatchdog.com: Bottom line, the best bit about this site is you can see both specific and "anywhere" discount flights from your departure city. That means that if you have some time to plan your travel, you can enter your destination, sign up for the e-mail alerts, and just wait for the deals to roll into your inbox. As a bonus, you can set price and fare type limits to get the most meaningful results.

Tripadvisor.com: As one of the go-to online travel destinations, Trip Advisor has flight, lodging, and attraction information as well as a growing community. When you search for any airfare, there is a checkbox right below the info that says "Get an alert when Destination 1 to Destination 2 air prices drop."

Airports

There are over a dozen airports in Puerto Rico, but you probably need only concern yourself with the three largest as these are your most likely options for arrival and inter-island travel.

San Juan, Carolina: Luis Muñoz Marin International Airport (SJU). If you are flying into Puerto Rico, chances are high that you are flying into this airport. It is by far the most active airport on the island and a stone's throw away from the popular San Juan Isla Verde hotels. It is a joint civilian/military airport and serves over 20 commercial airlines including the popular American, Delta, JetBlue, Southwest, United and US Airways. Here is the official website, with English selected as the main language: http://aeropuertosju.com/en. 787-253-2329 (main information center).

Aguadilla: Rafael Hernández International Airport (BQN). This airport serves JetBlue, United and Spirit airlines, with an expansion project in the works over the next decade or so. It serves an average of 51 passenger flights per week. 787-890-1680.

Ponce: Mercedita International Airport (PSE). Although it has served worked with other carriers in the past, it currently only services JetBlue which has regular service to Orlando, FL and JFK airport in New York City. 787-840-3151.

4. LODGING – DON'T DO
WHAT EVERYONE ELSE DOES

Poolside at the lovely San Juan Intercontinental Hotel.

Rules to Lodge By

Visit during the "off" or "shoulder" season. "Peak Season" is defined as November 30th-June 1st for the Caribbean, and is intended as a guideline to help travelers avoid hurricanes and enjoy the greatest portion of fair weather. However, weather is always a gamble, (particularly in the tropics!), so travelers who bet all their chips on the false peace of mind that peak season guarantees fair weather, do so at a financial premium.

The savvy vacationer who can travel off-season when hotels and airlines need to fill rooms and seats will likely take advantage of steep discounts. It's a gamble either way, but just how arbitrary the peak season guideline is will seem most obvious during the 'Off Season,' when a couple of weeks can mean the difference between a virtually empty hotel and one that is a beehive of activity. The same holds true for traffic, shopping, restaurant seating, parking, adventure tour openings, general noise and personal space. Wait, you mean you enjoy more while paying...LESS?!

Although there is a higher chance of hurricane season weather (rain, wind, possibly severe), here's what you get for traveling off season:

- A lot more money in your pocket for avoiding peak season premiums.
- A lot more space (and quiet!) at your <50% occupancy hotel.
- Less crowding at the local restaurants and attractions.
- Rare photo opportunities of famous places with no/few tourists.

Know what you're getting into. Have you heard of Oyster.com? Well we hadn't until before this trip. It's a great resource with independent, non-touched-up photos and reviews of hotels all over the globe. If you ever suspect that the hotel website *might* be using some camera filters and special lenses to make the rooms and grounds look nicer than they are, go find it on Oyster to get the real scoop. This is a great resource to help give you a more realistic picture (literally) of what to expect during your stay.

Talk to the hotel staff and other guests. People are full of interesting stories – all you have to do is introduce yourself and ask them a question. The staff at our hotel was extremely professional, minding their own business and focusing on their duties. Once asked a question, however, they really opened up and shared a wealth of information with us. We definitely got the 'inside scoop.' Hotel employees may be your first contacts on the island, and they can be an indispensable resource – we learned a lot from our hotel staff and got some great recommendations for a day trip. Just by asking!

You might think that staff might be tired of talking to vacationing mainlanders, but everyone we approached was sincere, open, and very helpful. And don't be shy about talking to other guests – people like to share stories. You might meet someone who knows about a fantastic restaurant, a great beach find, or who is just an interesting person to talk to!

Leave the hotel. The somewhat contrived experience that the tourism industry has created for you is available, but it isn't reality. After all, you didn't come all this way to buy a McBurger, did you? Do you want the same vacation photos as everybody else? Or do you want to have the kind of vacation experience that other people will only ever read about in a travel magazine?

Seriously, hit the road and explore the big beautiful island – it's brimming with surprises. In case you're thinking that you should work out at the hotel gym, enjoy some room service, and then treat yourself to a spa massage…you absolutely could (and you probably deserve it), but consider this alternative: have an amazing breakfast at a local pastry shop, go hiking on the beach, then take a rejuvenating oxygen bath high in the rainforest. You can go to a gym and spa when you get home!

Even if you don't have a plan, leave your hotel TV off, pack your day bag and get out – time in your room is time you're missing what the island has to offer. One of the best things about a nice, comfy hotel room is coming back to it *at the end of the day.*

It may sound like this defeats the purpose of booking a superb hotel but you may find the warm swimming pool and lavish bed will never feel better than after an action-packed day of sightseeing and road trips. As an added bonus, the thin "off season" crowds only get thinner after dark, and you may find yourself enjoying the pool and any other hotel perks with more space and privacy. Spending the day out and about made our time at the hotel even more special, because we made every moment count.

Enjoying the pool all to ourselves!

We were constantly amazed at how much of the beautiful hotel we had to ourselves. Because hotels have fewer guests during off-season, the evenings were very special – first a moonlit walk on the beach, followed by some night swimming in the amazing pool, and finished off with some quiet time in the hot tub. Cozy, romantic, and perfect!

Alternative Lodging Options

While a stay at a 5-star hotel has all the amenities you would expect, you may be craving something more off the beaten path. For those of you drawn to this option, here are three avenues you might explore:

AirBnB www.airbnb.com. An online directory of private residences available for lodging, there are over 1,000 listings for the island of Puerto Rico, with accommodations ranging from single shared rooms to entire private villas. As expected, most of the listings are located on the beaches but you might even find a mountain bungalow. You can often save money and possibly get to know your host via AirBnB and mitigate unpredictability via host reviews. Because this isn't your standardized hotel experience, it that can have its pros and cons. Make sure to review each property if you are considering going this route.

VRBO www.vrbo.com. VRBO stands for "vacation rentals by owner" and is similar to AirBnB, with more of the listings tending to be a bit more upscale and seemingly geared toward more private homes, condos and apartments versus rooms in shared spaces. They currently feature over 300 listings all across the island, even including some residences on Vieques and Culebra.

HomeAway www.homeaway.com. A similar online directory, but almost exclusively private (not shared) apartments, condos, and homes. This is actually a great route for family getaways, vacations for more than one couple or a group of friends. They boast over 2,000 listings for Puerto Rico, ranging from more modest properties at $100/night to luxury properties at over $800/night.

Hostels www.hostelworld.com. For the student or truly budget-conscious, hostels may be worth considering. Though there aren't as many options, it could really pay off to investigate if you choose to go this route – nightly stays usually range between $12 - $25/night and some hostels even have private room options as opposed to a dormitory environment. Unfortunately the nature of hostels seems to be hit-or-miss, with most having both good and not-so-good reviews. In Puerto Rico you'll find more selection in San Juan proper, with a few more hostels scattered across Culebra, Fajardo, Rincon and Vieques.

5. TRANSPORTATION –
TO RENT OR NOT TO RENT

Driving the island was both amazing and a little stressful.

Deciding Whether or Not to Rent a Car

At $30-$100/day (depending on the vehicle), you want to weigh whether renting a car makes sense for your vacation plans. Although a regional light rail system connecting San Juan and Caguas has been approved (called Novotren), for the time being transportation defaults to taxis, shared cars, buses, and your own private rental car.

Here are some factors to help you decide whether or not renting a car is the right option for you:

Renting a Car: Pros

- Freedom to try out off-the-beaten path eateries and cafés, every day of your stay.
- Freedom to take a day trip (or two or three), venturing out beyond the hotel district or your home base.
- Set your own schedule for any trips to popular activities.
- Although some tours offer transportation in shared ride vans, if you have sensitivity to motion sickness consider that these rides may be an hour of backseat riding on winding roads and you may not be very comfortable.
- If you have two or more people and one can help navigate it will make driving easier.

Renting a Car: Cons

- Driving in San Juan can be quite stressful (more on that in a bit).
- Road signs are in Spanish, so driving may be initially disorienting.
- Parking in the metro areas can be challenging.
- Unless you spend more for full coverage insurance and tolls you run the risk of body damage and unintentional toll fees.
- If you do not plan to venture out every day, you may not get your money's worth (although you could only rent on certain days of your stay)
- Time spent with the logistics of checking out and returning your car. Depending on timing and crowds, this can take up to an hour each instance.

Car Rental: What to Watch For

There are a lot of companies happy to rent a car to you. However, this was likely the largest stress point for us and we definitely made some mistakes that we hope to help you avoid.

Because the traffic is so very unpredictable in Puerto Rico, this is one area in which we definitely recommend getting every kind of coverage and option you can. Here are the most important tips:

1. **Don't book online with a debit card** – your transaction may go through but then you may have some trouble at the time of getting your car in person. Luckily we had a backup approved credit card with us and were able to sort things out.

2. **Get the insurance coverage, at all costs.** It will be worth it. Fender benders are commonplace and many of the cars on the island bear the evidence. Our car was "nudged" twice while parked at night and we were lucky that it went under the radar.

3. **Opt for the extra charge for getting toll road coverage.** Even if you don't plan to take any toll roads, some parts of the island are "spaghetti freeway central" and before you know it you will be in some turn-only or exit-only lane with no choice but to end up on a toll road.

4. **Maps and directions.** Our advice here is that you should have every kind of mapping system available, and plan out your route a little before you head out. Phone GPS? Check! iPad Maps? Check! Car GPS? Check! Printed map? Check! Maybe this sounds like a little neurotic over-preparation, but considering that you're in new territory and might not speak fluent Spanish, it's a good idea to have planned routes and alternate routes as well. Drivers: if you have a co-pilot, they will be your saving grace. You can focus on driving and they can be your trusty navigator.

Recommended Car Rental Companies

Overall, car rental companies get mixed reviews and possibly because Rico does see a lot of tourism, sometimes the customer service can be less than enthusiastic. As with many things, it depends on who you encounter so just realize the service side of car rental might be hit-or-miss. We had both good and not-so-good experiences with customer service.

One thing we noticed was that getting everything sorted could take a while, so bring your patience and maybe a cup of coffee. These agencies get overall positive marks, amid competition with much lower rankings.

Charlie Car Rental: Local, competitive prices, located on the strip of the Isla Verde hotels near the airport. www.charliecars.com. 787-728-2418.

Alamo Rent-a-Car: Has vehicles at the San Juan LMM airport so you don't have to shuttle to the lot. Reservations online to speed up the process. www.alamo.com. 787-791-1805.

Enterprise Rent-a-Car: There are multiple locations, but the one at the San Juan airport ranks better than the others. No shuttle needed, open 24 hours. www.enterprise.com. 787-253-3722.

Driving: Expect the Unexpected!

Something really interesting about traveling is noticing how the particular driving style is a cultural norm and is almost like learning a new language – the language of the road.

If you decide to rent a car, be aware that driving in Puerto Rico can be a stressful experience that you want to give your full attention to. Imagine you are playing a one of those video games where cars and people may jump in your path unexpectedly. It's not that the rules of the road are much different than what you may be used to. It's the driving style and nuance that takes a little getting used to.

Here are some things to watch out for:

Road conditions are variable. In general, most roads and freeways on the island are in good shape. However, we advise you to remain vigilant. Imagine your surprise while cruising on the freeway at 65mph when you hit a huge pothole or a 4" drop-off! It happened to us and it felt a little like a scene out of "The Dukes of Hazzard." You may take for granted that any road maintenance or hazard will be clearly marked with light reflective signage, but in Puerto Rico this is not always the case.

Lane changes are often not signaled. Again, this is clearly part of the driving culture that may take some getting used to. For your safety, you should assume everyone is about to change lanes. Note that some drivers switch lanes very quickly. To make matters more confusing, some drivers are signaling continuously for no apparent reason. If you look around at the cars, you'll see that many of them have dents and damage...perhaps this is the reason why.

Beware of other cars entering traffic. This seems obvious, but hear us out: if you see a car sticking its nose into traffic, don't rely on rules of common sense. Drivers will not always wait for an opening and in fact often pull into traffic regardless of the speed or distance of approaching cars. This gives the impression of cars appearing from nowhere. Think of how many times you heard someone describe an accident by saying, "They seemed to come from nowhere." Yeah, it can be like that.

Keep your distance. Drivers may unexpectedly stop in busy traffic, whether to let out a passenger, run into the pharmacy, or just have a roadside chat with a pedestrian, so just be on the lookout. And pedestrians are fairly confident considering the unpredictable traffic. Keep your eyes open at crosswalks as pedestrians will scarcely give you a glance before entering the roadway. Never, ever go on auto-pilot, and for the love of palm trees please don't do anything that could distract you while driving.

Streets can be narrow and crowded. While driving in Puerto Rico you'll get the impression that many populated areas grew organically from their centers before the widespread use of automobiles. Because these are some of the oldest cities in the Americas, this is actually true. Streets are often narrow and lined on both sides with businesses, restaurants, cafes, and residences. This makes for some lively sightseeing if you're a passenger, but you'll need to apply laser focus if you're the driver. Both vehicular and pedestrian traffic abound and you want everyone inside and outside of your vehicle to be safe!

Always Be Parking

So, you've avoided any fender benders, swerved around that pothole and now it's time to park the car and slowly peel your fingers from the steering wheel. There's only one problem – where do you park?!

Assuming you're staying at the popular San Juan strip hotels, most have valets and gated parking lots but if you don't want that to eat into your budget, plan on driving around looking for the privilege of paying for one or having the stroke of luck of finding the much-coveted street spot. Now you're avoiding accidents, potholes, pedestrians, AND looking for parking! Soon you'll learn to ALWAYS be looking for parking, even when you may not immediately need it.

Parking at Night. For the overwhelming majority of our time in Puerto Rico, we didn't worry about our car at all. The exception was at night. We heard whispers of carjacking before we arrived on the island, but that assumes you've broken the most basic anti-theft rule of all: Never Leave Valuables Displayed In Your Car. If you're in the city, it's only prudent to park in a well-lit spot at night no matter what country you're in. Of course the hotels have parking, but you will pay extra for this convenient option, (our hotel charged $25 per day). While you may wince at this, it's not necessarily a bad choice. Here's why…

The next logical place to park near a hotel is typically going to be along the main drag lined with various other hotels. If you can find a spot here, take it! It's convenient, and in San Juan the police are very good about keeping your car and its contents safe from theft along the main streets close to the hotels. The downside is that if you make the most of your time on the island and return to your hotel in the evening, it's likely that the most convenient parking will be long gone.

The third option is to park on a secondary street within reasonable walking distance from your hotel. Finding free parking there will be easier, but the streetlights might be further away, and the police patrols less frequent. We never saw evidence of break-ins even on the darkest streets we parked on. However, twice we noticed damage to our car from other drivers attempting to shoehorn into adjacent parallel parking. Certainly this could have happened on any street, but it might be the most compelling reason to pay for hotel parking.

Basic Driving Translation

As if you already didn't have enough to pay attention to while driving, you may also be faced with unfamiliarity of Spanish-language street and freeway signage. This is where our earlier map advice will come in handy. Below are just a few of the basic terms you should familiarize yourself with (alphabetized in Spanish for easy on-the-go reference):

Carril: Lane

Ceda: Yield

Derecho: Right

Entrada: Entrance

Este: East

Hacia: Toward

Izquierdo: Left

Norte: North

Oeste: West

Pare: Stop

Peatones: Pedestrians

Salida: Exit

Sur: South

Transito: One-way. There are a lot of one-way streets, so keep an eye out for the signs with an arrow indicating the direction of traffic.

Should you find yourself off course, you can always stop and ask for directions:

"¿Donde está…?" (DON-day eh-STAH) Means "Where is…" and you can fill in the blank.

"Estoy buscando ___, ¿me puede dirigir? (eh-STOY boos-CAHN-doh ___, meh PUEH-deh dee-dih-HEER?) Means "I'm looking for ___, can you direct me?"

With regard to tollways, definitely make sure to opt for the rental car coverage for these, as mentioned before. That way you will just go through the toll stations with the seal. The tollways will be labeled "Autoexpreso" and the toll stations are announced as "Estación de peaje" with the distance in kilometers marked so you know that you'll need to slow down ahead. Even though it's in Spanish, you can navigate on over to www.autoexpreso.com to familiarize yourself with some of the road signs.

Taxis, Buses and Trolleys

Taxis. The taxi fare system in Puerto Rico is regulated, so in theory you should be getting a standardized price regardless of carrier. In San Juan it's based on a location zone system for which the rates are updated frequently, so you may want to ask your cabbie up front: 1) what the estimated fare will be for your destination and 2) whether they accept your credit card if you won't be paying with cash.

Additionally, you should know that there are extra fees for luggage ($1/bag), calling the taxi ($1), more than five passengers ($2/pp) and a night charge ($1) from 10pm to 6:30am. As a sample rate, if you arrive in San Juan's Luis Muñoz Marin airport and take a taxi to the Old San Juan waterfront piers (~7.5 mi), the trip should average ~$20. If you go from the airport area to El Yunque National Forest (~30 mi), expect an average of ~$65.

Some taxi services include:

- Metro Taxis: 787-725-2870
- Major Cab Company: 787-723-1300
- Michael Taxi Service: 787-661-9694
- Luquillo Taxi & Tours: 787-513-7685 (Luquillo)

Buses. Buses all across the island are very inexpensive to ride (.75). However, their schedules are unreliable and you could find yourself waiting an hour or more at a bus stop. Additionally, the last stops vary anywhere from between 6:20 and 9:40pm. For maximum freedom and efficiency of your vacation time, this may not be the preferred option. Schedules are posted at every bus stop, and the bus system phone number is 787-250-6064, and you may ask for an English-speaking representative.

Old San Juan Free Trolley. If you are touring Old San Juan on foot (which we recommend), you can get some respite from walking by hopping on the free trolley. You could potentially see more of Old San Juan by covering more ground, but just be patient as sometimes the trolley is full and you'll have to wait until the next pass. Running from 7am -7pm M-F and 9am-7pm on the weekend, this is a great option for getting around Old San Juan, with the caveat that they do not adhere to a set schedule. But you can always walk to the next trolley stop if you get impatient.

You can find a trolley stop map here: www.sanjuantrolleys.com.

Ridesharing (Uber, Lyft)

According to online reports, the arrival of Uber caused quite a stir with the local taxi services, so you may want to do some timely research to check on updates. However, our understanding is this – Lyft does not have a significant presence but Uber does in and around San Juan.

For this reason, you may want to have backup transportation options especially if you plan to travel outside of San Juan, or at very early or late hours.

6. FOOD – DON'T EAT THAT, EAT THIS

Beautiful mural outside Platos Restaurant - San Juan, PR.

Fast Food Chains and Familiar Fare

When you first hit the ground in urban Puerto Rico, you might think the airline made a mistake. Where there are a lot of people, there are many of the corporations and businesses you are familiar with on the mainland. Don't be surprised to see McDonald's, Burger King, Wendy's, Subway, KFC (to name a few). Certainly in San Juan, the popular US chains are found all along the hotel strip. While you might be tempted to stop in for a quick snack, we suggest you resist this urge because knitted within the same streets lies so much amazing native cuisine.

If you're really set on finding a great Italian or sushi restaurant in Puerto Rico, you certainly can. However, consider that for your limited time on the island, you have only a certain number of meal opportunities to really get to know the local dishes, food combinations, flavors, and preparation styles. We strongly encourage you to delay sushi night until you get back home!

Local Cuisine

With a rich history of native Indians (the Taíno), Spanish influence and Caribbean cross-pollination (Cuba, Haiti, etc.) – Puerto Rico's cuisine is a rich blend of many influences. Their spices and seasonings are savory, spicy-hot, and in some cases pungent – garlic, coriander, annatto, cilantro, cumin. Fish is very popular, as are chicken and pork – often you'll find street carts selling fried meats for a quick snack. Also popular are island-grown fruits (papaya, coconut, plantain) and root vegetables (yucca, taro, yautia).

If you're vegetarian, there are a variety of deliciously seasoned savory dishes to explore. Like we did, you might develop a plantain affinity. It's not an addiction. Really, we can stop eating them any time. :-)

Here is an essential list of popular Puerto Rican menu items, with a description to just barely whet your appetite. Remember that each restaurant can have its own unique preparation of these classics:

- Mofongo – Fried green plantains mashed with pork cracklings or bacon, and served with vegetables and a broth.
- Asopao – Chicken or shellfish gumbo, usually a side. ("Sopa de" means "soup of")
- Bacalaitos – Fried codfish fritters, often an appetizer.
- Tostones – Twice-fried green plantain slices, flattened into rounds.
- Maduros – Fried ripe plantains. Though sweet, can be added to savory dishes as well as desserts.
- Beans and rice – Many, many varieties of this staple side dish, often flavored with garlic, onions, coriander and peppers as a "sofrito" base.
- Candied fruits and vegetables – look around for different varieties: sweet potato, guava, pumpkin, etc.

When it's time to eat out, make your restaurant meals special! Pick a place that you're excited about, then go when you can take the time to really enjoy it. Order nothing familiar and everything you are curious about, including dessert, (leftovers make a great occasional picnic snack to grab from your hotel fridge). Spend an hour or two.

Remember, you're having Caribbean food...IN THE CARIBBEAN! When you're done, you'll remember this meal for the rest of your life, and have a great story to tell when you get back.

NOTE: Zip over to the end of Chapter 9 for a guided food tour recommendation.

Restaurant Notes and Resources

Before we dive into this section, we have to be completely up front about something. While we would absolutely love to share a list of restaurant reviews, the truth is that we are vegan and that means we can't offer reviews of full meal selections to appeal to the majority of readers. That said, there is one place that we found reliably good whose non-vegetarian menu items sounded creative and appetizing.

It was Café Berlin in Old San Juan. With a cozy atmosphere, friendly service and delicious food, Café Berlin is a reliable stop for good food and drinks. Located on Calle San Francisco just west of Norzagaray, their phone number is (787) 722-5205. Visit www.CafeBerlinPR.com for more details.

So considering individuals' specialized diets (including our own), the variety in personal food preferences, and the constant changes in the restaurant scene we decided you'd be best served by exploring the standard resources to cater to your unique inclinations. We've included some personal tips we've learned to use over the years as well.

Yelp.com – This review site is indispensible for travel. In addition to contributions by the locals, many who have come before you have taken the time to write reviews of their experiences from the perspective of a traveler. All of this information will be extremely helpful in saving you time, money, and helping you find exactly what you are looking for. Make sure to get the mobile app and put it on your phone and/or tablet. It's a fantastic way to get the lowdown on eateries that are close to your location and search by types of cuisine or dining, e.g. "vegetarian," "coffee shop," "beach." Here are two tips to help you out further:

Call the restaurant before going! We were excited to go to one place only to find out (after walking around the block a few times) that it had gone out of business.

Check via website or phone for hours of operation – sometimes restaurants are closed during slow hours and it is not reflected on the Yelp app.

TripAdvisor.com – Another great online review community that can help you make informed decisions. You can search for restaurants in the Puerto Rico city you're visiting right from the home page. Here are a couple of notes that we'd like to share:

Look at the photos submitted by visitors just like you, so that you can get a much better feel for the atmosphere. (not just "staged" photos.)

For the best information we recommend you sort by date (newest first). Often the restaurant management will take steps to remedy sources of complaints/dissatisfaction – so old, negative ratings may not be relevant anymore. And keep an eye out for replies to the comments – really involved management will read the reviews and post a reply.

Hotel concierge and staff – Keep in mind that hotel employees might be most inclined to promote their own restaurants (which we're sure are perfectly lovely), so you may want to phrase a question like this: "We'll be visiting [share area you'll be exploring] this morning/afternoon/evening – are there any restaurants in this area that you go to?" If you can, press the issue of places that they themselves would eat so that they don't give you the "popular with tourists" answer.

Groceries

The food in Puerto Rico is so delicious that we encourage you to do some restaurant homework, read reviews and be daring! That said, if you're looking to employ a cost-conscious strategy for your dining, you can absolutely have one or two meals out and the rest in your hotel or as a picnic.

For example, if you are OK with a light breakfast, coffee and some fruit at the hotel may tide you over until lunch. Try to keep snacks like fresh fruit, granola bars and plantain chips while out and about, because you can be more deliberate about dining choices instead of stopping in just anywhere because you're "SO HUNGRY!"

Here is a list of grocery stores you can find:

- SuperMax <-- this was our go-to grocery shop. Their website is in Spanish, but this hyperlink will take you to their locations page. Here is the main link: www.supermaxonline.com.
- Pueblo Supermarkets
- Amigo
- Grande

Snack Ideas

You may be surprised to see that many of your favorite snacks are available on the island. So, while you already know how to snack, there are few things we'd recommend you grab specifically for Puerto Rican adventures.

In addition to your standard bananas, apples, oranges and trail mixes, beyond the granola bar and sports drink, you may want to consider picking up plantain chip snacks some local fruits such as guava and tamarind pods.

Tamarind what? Pods. Tamarind pods. You can ask for them by name in Spanish: "tamarindo" (tah-mah-REEN-doh). Unlike in the states where the pods are very dry, they are in abundance on the island and the seeded pods are thick, sweet, and tart. They are delicious and a perfectly portable source of calories, so make sure to keep them handy. Since they are easily shelled and de-veined, you will want to keep a wet-nap or some kind of hand cleaner around so you're not left sticky.

A tip on water: If you have a hydro-pack (recommended), fill the bladder up with ½ ice and ½ water before you head out. The cool backpack will keep you and the water cool as the afternoon heats up.

7. THE BEACHES VS. THE MOUNTAINS

Postcard-perfect beach in Potala Pastillo near Ponce, PR.

Everyone loves the beach, right?

Well, we haven't conducted a formal poll but feel pretty confident that most everyone does. There's jut something magical and elemental about having the big blue ocean at your feet, and immersing yourself in something so vast. The sound of the surf, warm sand between your toes, and warm sun on your back. Ahhh…

Puerto Rico has plenty of beaches because technically, it is lined with them. ;) But seriously, possibly the most popular are at San Juan – no surprise, since this city houses the most popular airport and is also a regular port for the major cruise lines.

The Isla Verde beaches near the main San Juan hotel strip are perfectly lovely. During the off season they weren't crowded at all and although we witnessed brief rain showers, overall the weather was sunny and beach-perfect. NOTE: As a romantic option, a beach stroll at night is a great way to enjoy the breeze and crashing surf without having to slather yourself with sunblock.

Even though the more popular beaches are great, we absolutely encourage you to explore other beaches – you can drive less than two hours in pretty much any direction and hit a beach!

Here we describe some of the most popular beaches so you can decide which will suit you best:

Ocean Park Beach (San Juan): Tends to see more adults than families (translation: great for singles), and is reported to be a great beach for people watching and relaxing.

Rincón, Isabella, and Aguadilla Beaches: Hands-down the best for surfing in the winter months when the waves are at their highest. Favorite beaches in this area include: Sandy Beach, Crash Boat Beach, and Domes Beach.

It's worth noting that some of the best-reviewed beaches are on the nearby islands of Culebra and Vieques. More detail on that in Chapter 11: Day Trips.

Favorite beaches in Culebra include: Flamenco Beach, Zoni Beach, Flamingo Beach, and Tamarindo Beach.

Favorite beaches in Vieques include: Caracas Beach, Secret Beach, Media Luna Beach, and Navio Beach.

You can ask your concierge or host for their personal favorites. Oh, and before you pack, you may want to review the Beach Vacation Packing List (http://bit.ly/BeachList) we compiled especially for this occasion to make sure you don't forget anything.

The Mountains

High up in the mountains as we traverse the island on Hwy 52.

As anyone who has lived near a mountain range will tell you, mountains are kind of magical – and even more so in a subtropical climate where literally every square inch is covered with life.

So we're going to step out on a very mossy limb here and come right out and say it: we were a little bit more enchanted with the mountains than with the oceanfront. Both are amazing, but if we HAD to pick…we'd definitely be in higher altitudes.

Here are some of the things we loved about the mountains:

- Almost no tourists
- Beautiful scenery
- Cooler temperatures
- Mysterious misty areas
- EVERYthing is green
- Amazingly scenic drives

You'll find more detail on El Yunque National Rainforest in Chapter 10. In addition to the required visit to El Yunque, we also wanted to mention one other excursion.

Guajataca Forest Reserve: Nearest the city of Isabela, this reserve gets rave reviews for being out of the way and featuring the impressive Wind Caverns with many stalactite and stalagmite formations. You can find more detail by searching for this reserve on TripAdvisor.com.

Our speed was more along the lines of hiking and exploring, but the mountains also offer climbing, zip-lining and rappelling for the more adventurous.

8. STEPPING BACK IN TIME –
THE NATIONAL HISTORIC SITE

Introduction and Notes for Chapters 8-12

There is a countless array of things you can do and see in Puerto Rico. This list isn't meant to exclude activities, nor is it the result of formal surveys or popular travel magazine results. They are prioritized based on personal experience blended with the following criteria:

- Specific to Puerto Rico, not found elsewhere.
- Good for singles, couples, groups, and families.
- Offers natural environmental beauty.
- An enjoyable and fun experience (photo opportunities a bonus).
- Memorable and something you might want to do again.

Bonus Resources: As mentioned earlier, an e-book can't play songs or videos for you, nor can it offer a full range of photos without creating a massive download file, but....the Internet can! To that end, we have created an online Puerto Rico Resource Portal (http://bit.ly/PRportal) to enhance your exploration, which includes:

- In-depth photo essays for Old San Juan, El Yunque, and the Inner Loop day trip
- Videos of Cristobal Castle and Bio Bay
- Traditional Puerto Rican food recipes
- An overview (with video) on the national mascot who will serenade you nightly
- A video introduction to Puerto Rico's music genres

- A photo essay on Puerto Rico's pristine deserted island
- With more to be added...

Just click the link above or visit www.happyholidaysguides.com and select "Puerto Rico" under "Destinations." There's no catch, we simply felt compelled to share multimedia resources for a more in-depth exploration of Puerto Rico.

Additional Guided Activities, with Booking Links:

For convenience, you may want to book activities where you have a guide and don't have to worry about transportation – great options if you're not renting a car.

We've culled some options for consideration if you want to go this route. Please keep in mind that sometimes the difference between a great and bad experience with a tour company can depend on the tour guide's mood, logistical issues, and a number of other factors. For this reason, we encourage you to read the reviews, price-compare, and read all included/excluded fees and terms before booking.

Separately, we've provided links for booking and research convenience – *please* try to suspend judgment as some of the websites aren't exactly slick or modern. Despite appearances, these agencies have been operating successful tours with satisfied customers.

And now, let's step back in time to the Spanish military outpost in Old San Juan...

View between the historic El Morro and Cristobal Castle Forts.

National Historic Site Overview

This historic site is located on the northwest edge of Old San Juan. It was constructed by the Spanish beginning in 1539 and is comprised of two castles and a long beachfront fortification wall. Over the years it served to protect the island from British, Dutch, and U.S. attack.

Today, even if you aren't into history, it is a beautiful site to explore.

The site is open every day from 9-6pm except major holidays. Park rangers offer orientations every hour, and a short film is also available. At Cristobal Castle, there are tunnel and outer defense tours at 10:30 am and 2:30 pm, respectively. El Morro offers a lighthouse tour and talk at 10:30 am. Visit the National Park Service website at www.nps.gov as they sometimes have special events on the calendar and offer after-hours tours (or simply search for "San Juan" from the nps.gov website).

Cost and Time

Admission to both fortresses is $3 separately or a mere $5 for both, and kids under 15 get in free. This price includes all-day access (save your receipt), and even a free tram between castles. This deal is impossible to beat!

You could technically drive up to Cristobal Castle, zoom around the grounds taking a few pictures then take the trolley over to El Morro and do the same in under two hours.

However, to truly take in the architecture, history and vistas, we suggest spending more time here.

Recommended Path

If played right, a visit to the historic site can be an entire rewarding morning or afternoon on its own – one with a variety of scenery ranging from the historic to epic views of both the coastline and Old San Juan. As a bonus, you'll even get to stretch your legs and mingle with the locals.

You can start your experience at either castle, but Cristobal Castle offers much-coveted parking in the NPS lot, so we recommend starting here. The NPS charges a reasonable rate for this privilege, but oddly, you must return to the visitor center and request to be charged. Gates lock at 5pm.

If starting at Cristobal, your tour begins via a cool, dark, cavernous passageway which emerges into the main courtyard of the fort. From here you can explore at will. The NPS has recreated various aspects of 16th century tropical military outpost life, including fully stocked sleeping quarters and information on how the water system worked. Much has changed in 400 years but this site is quite well preserved.

Yet what surely haven't changed are the stunning views from atop the castle(s). As one might expect from a naval fortress, the panoramic coastal vistas are some of the most breathtaking on the island. Looking back towards Old San Juan is similarly impressive. History, ocean, and modern city all intersect at this unique location.

Photo Opportunity

Some of the most spectacular photos of your trip can be found atop Cristobal Castle. The fortress isn't going anywhere, so you have all the time you need to set up eye-popping shots. If your camera has a 'panorama' setting, this is the time to use it! Although it will look small on this page, here is a sample:

Remember we mentioned how we wanted to offer resources beyond the limitations of an e-book? You can find a video tour of Cristobal Castle on our Puerto Rico Resource Portal (http://bit.ly/PRportal).

After an hour or two at Cristobal, we advise that you skip the shuttle and walk the scenic 0.9 miles west to Castillo Del Morro if you can. Follow Calle Norzagaray roughly along the old city wall (you spill onto this as you exit Cristobal Castle). The street is lined with quaint oceanview residences. Soak in their heady charm while you can because the land beneath them seems destined for condos and trendy shops. On your right is the ocean. As you stroll along, stop at any of the former bastions (now converted to parks), for a peek of the surf below.

ROMANTIC INTERLUDE

Eventually the street will lead you to the immense El Morro park. This expansive grass-carpeted park is a destination in its own right, and you will find many locals spending a weekend afternoon there to have a picnic or fly a kite, (the coastal breeze is perfect for this). We recommend you do likewise.

Great spot for a picnic or impromptu kite-flying.

Adjacent to El Morro park on the edge of the water is Cementerio Maria Magdelena De Pazzis, a nineteenth century cemetery containing beautifully ornate memorial stones and statues of Puerto Rico's most prominent residents. This is definitely worth a stop, especially since it sits between you and San Felipe De Morro Castle.

Safety Note: The cemetery is adjacent to the La Perla neighborhood, which online accounts report is best to avoid, especially at night. We didn't see any suspect activity, but it is a bit run down and plentiful with graffiti…best to walk down from the castle grounds.

Maria Magdalena de Pazzis Cemetery.

After a mile of scenery, you're ready to get back to the business of exploring castles, or at least enjoy having completed the 360° panorama of the fort complex. Having satisfied all your historical curiosities and appetite for natural beauty, it's time to head back to the NPS parking lot at San Cristobal. *NOW* you can hop on the free tram. The only thing is that hardly a single person may get off to afford you a seat. No worries, you're on island time! Just take in the sights and sounds all the way back to Cristobal Castle. It's less than a mile so a great way to work in a leisurely stroll.

Optional Guided Activities

This exploration is better at your own pace and arriving at the gates from San Juan is an easy drive or taxi ride away. For these reasons, the only guidance you may want is to watch for the times for the guided park ranger tours listed above so that you can get a better view into the history of the site. While tour agencies do offer guided outings, for this particular activity we don't see sufficient added value from paying a commercial tour agency when the park rangers offer free tours.

9. THE MAGIC OF OLD SAN JUAN

View of Old San Juan from atop a historic fort wall.

Old San Juan Overview

San Juan was founded in 1509, making for some beautiful architecture on the historic buildings, and an Old World feel of narrow cobblestone streets.

If you have an appreciation for traditional colonial style architecture, you'll definitely want to make time to see this part of the city. However, something to be aware of is that the heat, humidity, narrow streets, and hills are better for a leisurely stroll than a brisk walk. You definitely will need comfortable shoes, light clothing, and a good map so you can identify spots where you'd like to stop in for a drink or snack.

Ladies: if you can at all find a hand fan, you will be the envy of the city. Separately, take into consideration that all of the cruise ships disembark here, so it's very possible to hit some large crowds depending on your timing.

Cost and Time

If you are driving, you will most likely need to allow about $15 for parking in one of the garages which are concentrated on the south side (make sure to take cash as some machines do not accept cards.) Other than that, any spending for food or shopping is strictly discretionary for any food and shopping you may want to participate in. You might want to allow about $10 - $15 for a nice sit-down meal and a little extra for any alcoholic beverages.

As far as how much time to spend, we recommend at least a half-day for leisurely strolling and enjoying the arts, crafts all the stores have to offer. If you plan to admire the architecture, stop in at the small city parks to relax, wander into different stores for local arts and coffees, you can easily spend the full day taking in the sights. Keep in mind you can hop on and off the free trolley as noted in Chapter 6, using the map as a guide.

This is a great place to meander about, shop, and people-watch. You may wander onto different parks, sculpture, and hidden gems as you explore, and following is just one suggestion that proved a delightful route.

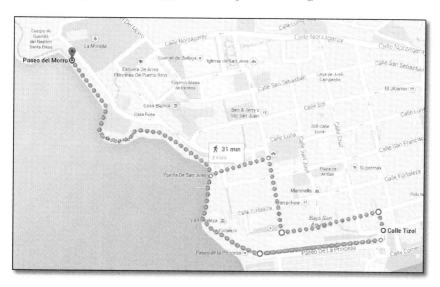

Paseo del Morro to Paseo de la Princesa, Image ©Google.

Recommended Path

For a great scenic walk, begin at Paseo del Morro, which you can access by heading west on Caleta de San Juan such that you arrive at the **Puerta de San Juan** ("San Juan Door") at the coastline. From there you can walk south until you get to Paseo de la Princesa. There are plenty of benches and spectacular trees, so there is no need to rush.

As you reach the end of the Paseo heading eastward now, you will reach the beautiful **Raíces Fountain**, we suggest you sit down to watch people bustle about. Just north of the fountain is a popular spot for fairs and exhibits so you may find some arts and crafts or other event occupying this space, especially if you go on a weekend.

From here you can walk north on Calle Tizol, then head west on Calle Tetual. When that street ends you'll be at the **Plaza las Palomas**, literally "Pigeon Park." One side of this park is a large red brick wall with lots of little pigeon cubby holes in it, usually housing 1-3 pigeons in each. You can buy some cracked corn from a local vendor there, but more than likely the park will be covered in corn so these are probably the best-fed pigeons on the island. Kids will likely get a kick out of this, and as an adult it's worth a 10-minute stop for the novelty.

Heading north from Pigeon Park you'll hit Calle Fortaleza, which on its west end will take you directly to **La Fortaleza** ("The Fortress"), a UNESCO World Heritage site which was completed in 1540 and has been an executive political mansion ever since, now home to Puerto Rico's governor. For just $3 you can take the guided tour inside and explore the chapel, dungeon and gardens. Tours are available 9am-4pm Monday through Friday.

The Raíces Fountain at the east end of Paseo de la Princesa.

This recommended path can take you over an hour if you stop and smell the roses, which is the best way to enjoy it.

NOTE: You can find more Old San Juan photos in a photo essay we've published online: http://bit.ly/TTDsjpr.

Optional Guided Activities in San Juan

Guided Tour Disclaimer: Friends, please consider the prices we list as a guideline only – pricing changes frequently depending on season, date, and market demand. Always visit the websites or call the tour guides to make sure you don't get any surprises.

Old San Juan Food Tour

Perfect for foodies who want a taste of the real Puerto Rico.

Viator's Old San Juan Food Tour: Transportation not included. Walking tour of six different restaurants. Can accommodate most dietary restrictions. 3 hours, $78 pp. Learn more at www.viator.com.

Other Tours

Segway Tours of Puerto Rico: If zipping around on a Segway is more your speed, you can book a tour of the historic site (2-hr, $93) or cruise around key Old San Juan attractions (:45, $42). 787-598-9455. Learn more at https://www.segwaytourspr.com.

Night Tales in Old San Juan: A 2-hour evening guided walking tour where you will visit different historic landmarks and hear stories about film stars, prisoners, and the military. 787-605-9060. Learn more at http://www.hellotourguide.com/old_san_juan_night_walking_tour.html

10. EL YUNQUE NATIONAL FOREST

Amazingly dense El Yunque Rainforest path.

El Yunque Overview

In our opinion, El Yunque is a must-see. Sure, there are hundreds of square miles of tropical forest in Puerto Rico. So what makes this a special trip?

Simply put, El Yunque is the one place in Puerto Rico with a convenient combination of everything you could possibly need or want when exploring the rainforest; smooth roads, parking, bathrooms, picnic/camping facilities, scenic jungle accessible by an extensive trail system, and fantastic mountain views. All of this within an environment managed by federal park rangers, should you need one.

El Yunque is part of the U.S. National Park Service and sees 1.25 million visitors per year. As with any tourist attraction, the vast majority of these come during peak season. Off-season travelers may find the park quiet enough for a trailside nap. Sure, there will be other people around, but the majesty of the park tends to instill inner (and outer) silence. If you want to simply drive up and find a spot or trailhead, you can.

Occasionally, the forest experiences landslides that may block off parts of the road or trails. You can check under "Alerts and Notices" on the El Yunque section of the USDA website for the latest, here: http://www.fs.usda.gov/elyunque.

Cost and Time

If you stop at the visitor center you are asked for $3 per person, $5 if you would like a park ranger tour. Oh, and camping is free, though you'll need a permit. No matter how you look at it, it's a fantastic deal. If you are interested in easy to moderate hiking, you can have a great experience during just a morning or afternoon visit. We suggest going in the morning in case you fall in love and plan to spend more time or if you want to hike the more challenging trails – it's a good idea to pack a lunch just in case.

First, a picturesque view from the El Yunque observation tower, and a close-up of a little friend we ran into – notice even the snail is covered in life (algae!).

The way in is also the way out, so you will drive up, climbing in elevation, until you can go no further and have to turn around.

While you will want to get a trail map and explore along paths which are suited to your agility level – they are marked as easy, intermediate or strenuous – there are definitely a couple of things you will without doubt want to enjoy.

Recommended Path

For an easy exploration of El Yunque you needn't stray too far from the main drive (State Road 191). Not too long after you pass the visitor center, you will see **La Coca Falls** cascading down on your right, and under the road on your left. Keep an eye out for the parking area so you can get the requisite "this is me in front of the waterfall" photo. From here, driving up just a short way you will see the trailhead for **La Coca Trail** on your left. Walk past the picnic tables along the parking lot and hike down just a little way. There you will find an old cement shelter enveloped by the jungle. It will have a table and fireplace, making for a surreal picnic spot.

When you are ready to jump back in your car, up a little ways will be **The Yokahú Observation Tower on your left.** The old circular stone tower has its own parking area, so you should be able to find a spot and just walk on over. Inside the tower you'll climb up a winding staircase a few stories up and emerge onto a lovely observation deck. In the distance to the north you can see the city of Rio Grande – this deck is a great place to snap lots of pictures.

For a nice beginner hike, you can drive up a little further and walk along the **Caimitillo Trail**. It's easy to navigate, although since everything is wet, be mindful of slippery surfaces. Now, this trail does connect with the more demanding **El Yunque Trail**, which will take you to the dizzying peak at an elevation of 3,461 feet. When you feel like you are done you can simply backtrack.

Other points of interest on easier trails include **La Mina Falls** as well as **El Baño Grande** lagoon. For the intrepid, of course there's the **El Yunque Peak** as well as the **Mt. Britton** observation tower.

ROMANTIC INTERLUDE

Keep an eye out for sitting areas which may have 2 - 3 benches under a covered roof. These are along some of the trails and are a fantastic spot to stop, sit, breathe deeply of the oxygen-rich air and just be amazed that you are sitting amidst such unspoiled beauty. Taking just 5 minutes to sit, breathe, and listen to the forest sounds is just as valuable as all the lovely pictures you're sure to take.

NOTE: You can find additional photos of the El Yunque Forest in this photo essay published online: http://bit.ly/YunqueNF.

Additional Guided Tours to El Yunque

If you decide not to rent a car, there are definitely options for getting to El Yunque, which, in our opinion, you don't want to miss. Here are a few guided options that include transportation.

Viator's El Yunque Half-Day Tour: Includes transportation from select San Juan hotels. Guided walking/hiking tour through El Yunque key tourist points. 5.5 hours, from ~$66 pp. Learn more at www.viator.com.

Viator's El Yunque and Luquillo Beach Full-Day Tour: In addition to the above forest tour, you will also spend some time in nearby Luquillo Beach, which you can see off in the distance from the top of the observation tower. It's a great place to relax and have a snack or some drinks. 8 hours, $92 pp. This comes out to be less than $12 an hour and is a pretty great deal for a complete day trip. Learn more at www.viator.com.

11. DAY TRIPS –
SEEING THE REAL PUERTO RICO

Mountain driving. Yes, those are bamboo canes.

If you're willing to spend a day off the beaten path (and we hope you are), there are various scenic drives convenient from San Juan. This is possibly the BEST way to view the island. Go where tourists are not expected, and you'll be guaranteed an authentic Puerto Rican experience, whether it's food, towns/cities, or simply people-watching.

We'll share several island day trips with you, both guided and on your own. We'll begin with our favorite (we took the adventurous route and can vouch for the amazing scenery).

An Inner Loop Around the Island

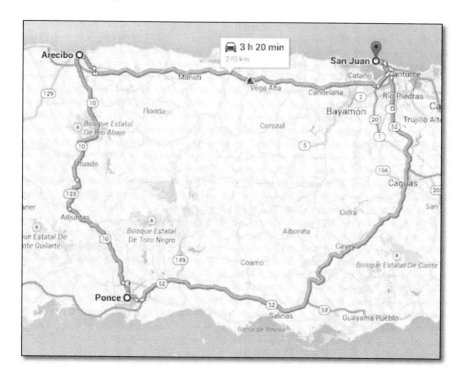

Inner Loop Day Trip, Image ©Google Maps

This road trip has it all: towns, cities, coastline, and jungle. It can be done in a day, making it a must-do for anyone interested in experiencing a remarkable cross section of the real Puerto Rico. Although the route is a fairly simple highway-to-highway jaunt, you'll be amazed at both the diversity and sheer beauty this trip reveals. We recommend getting started early for this trip.

The route is Hwy 52 Tollway south to Ponce, Hwy 10 Freeway north to Arecibo, then Hwy 22 Tollway back to San Juan. Although Google calculates the travel time at approx. 3 hrs and 20 minutes for 380km or 167 miles, the reality is that it doesn't take road conditions into consideration. For example, much of the highway on the first leg of your trip will be interrupted with traffic lights. Driving up in the mountains will be slow as you coil your way between jungle towns. Combine these with lunch, all the quaint scenery and spectacular views you will want to photograph, and it makes for a very long day. It will also be one of the highlights of your trip, guaranteed.

If you begin your journey from San Juan by heading south on the Highway 52 tollway, it may be slow going for the first couple hours, particularly on weekdays when many people are heading off to work. The stop and go freeway traffic will be somewhat rewarded by the greenery and interesting sites around you, however. Once through Caguas, you'll begin to pick up speed and should be able to blaze a trail all the way to Ponce before lunchtime. OK, considering your gaze might be drawn by the beautiful scenery, you shouldn't be blazing too fast, but you'll certainly encounter less traffic.

A Note for the Especially Adventurous: For an experience of more mountain majesty and getting a peek at real mountain living, you may take the parallel 2-lane highways north and south. That is, taking Hwy #1 freeway southbound and Hwy #123 freeway northbound. Zooming in on a map you can see multiple zig-zagging switchbacks on both roads.

This route will add time to your journey and requires quite a bit of attention and patience due to the narrow road and sharp turns. However, you will be privy to some truly amazing scenery, mountain homes, and a surreal feeling of cutting a swath right through the heart of the mountainous jungle. We realize this is not for everyone (certainly not anyone prone to carsickness) but for those who can tolerate it, you can imagine what the first Spanish settlers must have thought stumbling into this paradise.

Coffee Break: If you're starting out in San Juan, consider taking a quick break *before* you venture into Ponce. The drive from San Juan can be a bit fatiguing, and you'll need to be sharp and on your game before Ponce traffic puts you to its test. Located a couple streets off the highway, Con Leche Coffee Bar & Bistro offers good coffee, pastry, and sandwiches at very reasonable prices. This place is popular with locals. Always a good sign! Check them out on Yelp!

Ponce is named after Ponce de León, so it is the "City of Lions."

When in Ponce: You can stop in at the **Plaza las Delicias** main town square and enjoy a snack by the central fountain while you look at all the colorful lion statues. Then you can stroll over to the **Our Lady of Guadeloupe Cathedral** to marvel at the intricate architecture. You can also visit the **Parque de Bombas** firefighters' museum that used to be a fully functioning firehouse. Painted in red and black stripes (the city colors) this building is impossible to miss.

If you want to wander out past the main plaza, a popular destination and great lunch spot is the **La Guancha** boardwalk in Barrio Playa. With over 20 kiosks, flanked by beaches, and lots of boats within view, this is a good place to relax for lunch or a refreshing drink. There is also a children's park nearby and an observation tower you can climb for novel views.

Planning advice: This is an amazing drive, no question. That said, you are in unfamiliar territory with possibly unfamiliar road signs, so here are some notes to help you plan:

- Take multiple maps and map backups – ideally GPS so you can check if you're on course since you could easily miss your exit to the right highway when you're the city.
- Leave early for ample time to explore and possibly get back to your hotel before sundown – the twists and turns in the inner mountains are numerous and you want to be fully alert for safety.
- Check the weather report. If rain is expected, allow more time for delays and for safe driving.
- Have a hearty breakfast and pack plenty of road snacks and water just in case you're not near roadside convenience stores or groceries.

NOTE: You can find additional photos of the inner loop day trip excursion in this photo essay published online: http://bit.ly/PRiloop

Unlike the attractions closer to San Juan, chartered trips to Ponce are a little harder to come by, although here is one for consideration.

Rico Sun Tours Colonial Ponce Tour also offers a tour from San Juan, you can simply check their website for availability. $110 pp. Call for details: 787-722-2080. Learn more at www.rstpuertorico.com.

Additional Day Trip Options: Guided or On Your Own

If you decide not to rent a car, that doesn't mean you have to be confined to your hotel or home base. Although you will need to concede to the tour schedules, one advantage is that you don't have to worry about fighting traffic or getting lost.

Arecibo Observatory and Rio Camuy River Cave Park Exploration Day Trip. This is an excellent option for the science-minded and nature-lovers. The Arecibo Observatory is the world's largest single-dish radio telescope, although it may lose that title soon to the new one being built in China. Here are two interesting facts about this station: 1) It is constantly scanning for signs of intelligent extraterrestrial life (the SETI project); and 2) It made a cameo appearance in 007's Goldeneye movie, so you if you're a James Bond fan you may recognize it from there.

The Camuy river is the world's 3rd-largest underwater river. Its caves have been around for over 1 million years, and they are still being mapped! You'll see sinkholes, stalactites and maybe even some bats!

If you DO have your own transportation, plan on a full day for this delightful science-lover's excursion. The **Arecibo Observatory** is only open Wed - Sunday from 9am-4pm. Adults $10, children & seniors $6. http://www.naic.edu. 787-878-2612.

The **Rio Camuy Cave Park** is also only open Wed-Sun, but from 8:30am to 5pm (last tour at 3:30pm). The tour is about 1.5 hrs. Entrance fees for adults are $15, kids 4-10 are $10 (free under 4) and allow $5 for parking. KM 19 at Route 129. 787-898-3100.

Catamaran Snorkel and Picnic Cruise to Icacos Island. If you want to spend most of the day on the water, exploring a semi-pristine beach with a small group of people, this will be a good option for you. This guided cruise includes ground and water transportation (from select San Juan hotels), lunch, beverages and snorkel equipment. It departs early and returns late afternoon, in time for you to have dinner on your own and relax. Icacos island, off the coast of Fajardo on the east side, is uninhabited and a protected nature reserve, so you will be assured clear waters and a very private experience. Viator's Snorkel Cruise offers this day tour (8.5 hrs) starting at $83 pp. Learn more at www.viator.com.

Day Trips to Vieques and Culebra Islands. Vieques and Culebra islands are world-renown for their white sands and clear azure waters, both lying to east of Fajardo. If you have your own car, you can drive to the Fajardo ferry dock and take the "lancha" across. The dock is located at the end of Hwy 195, which you can access by Hwy 3 heading eastward from San Juan, Rio Grande, or Luquillo. Because your ticket will only be about $5 round trip plus $5 for parking, this is a very affordable option. However, some considerations are:

- The ferry will not always leave on time…they may be early or late.
- You generally cannot make reservations in advance.
- Your desired departure time may be sold out.
- If you're late, your place may be sold to someone else, and you don't want to be stranded out on the islands faced with an unplanned overnight stay.
- Most car rental companies will not allow you to take your car over on the cargo ferry.
- The ferry trip can take up to 1.5 hours each way, with only 4 departures per day.

- You should arrive 1-2 hours early to make sure you get the seat and departure time you are hoping for.

These are not densely populated islands so they do not run like efficient tourism machines. Phones may go unanswered, hours and prices may change at will…some patience is required.

Here is a ferry schedule with phone numbers: https://vieques.com/ferry-vieques-fajardo/

Barring the ferry, you can also fly there based on select locations via Vieques Air Link. Learn more at: https://www.viequesairlink.com/

Vieques Fast Facts:

- Home to two bioluminescent bays, including Mosquito Bay.
- Is underdeveloped (there are no traffic lights) though becoming a more popular tourist destination.
- Once used by the US Navy for weapons testing, these activities were halted by protests and now much of the island serves as a wildlife refuge.

Unless you have a planned tour near the port, you will need to rent a car for access to the island's best beaches on the south side. Avis now offers online booking for Vieques, whereas the other agencies require reservations by phone or in person.

If you arrive in Vieques via the ferry port, taxis should be available to take you to your destination. Here are some activity options.

Ahoy! Vieques Sailing Charters: If you want to enjoy charted sailing with a small group, you may book ½ day to full day. From ~$135 per person. Learn more at www.viequessailingcharters.com.

Island Adventures BioBay Eco-Tours: Enjoy all the wonders of a bioluminescent bay. NOTE: Unless you are booking the guided tour in Chapter 12 which will take you back to Fajardo, you should make plans for one night of accommodations on Vieques island. Tour runs about $50 per person, $35 for children. 787-741-0720. Learn more at www.biobaytourvieques.com.

Abe's All-in-One Snorkeling and Bio Bay Tour: If you are in Vieques, this 6-hour tour has a little bit of everything: kayaking, swimming, snorkeling, lunch and of course the bioluminescent Mosquito Bay at night.

$150 per person ($100 per child). 787-741-2134. Learn more at www.abessnorkeling.com.

There is a catamaran Vieques Bio Bay tour that will take you back to Fajardo on the main island, which is listed in the next chapter.

Culebra Fast Facts:

- "Isla de Culebra" means "Snake Island."
- Culebra is flanked by 23 smaller islands off of its coast, most of which are nature reserves.
- Permanent population hovers around only 2,000 people – so expect a laid-back environment and "island time."
- It does have a small airport - Benjamin Rivera Noriega Airport - serviced by Vieques Air Link (mentioned earlier), Flamenco Air (787-741-1040) and Isla Nena Air (888-263-6213).

From the ferry dock, you may catch a shuttle bus to Flamenco Beach, which has been consistently rated one of the most beautiful beaches in the world for its white sands and unspoiled beauty.

Culebra Eco-Tours Jet Ski Tour: $160 for 1 or 2 people on one jet ski. This 2-hour tour around the island includes the guide's instruction on the ecosystem, wildlife sightings, and one or two stops for a swim. 787-902-7928.

12. BIOLUMINESCENT BAYS
LIGHT UP THE NIGHT!

Bio Bays Overview

First off, just because this section is at the end and doesn't have a picture doesn't mean it's not COMPLETELY SPECTACULAR. Because it is. However, since it's a night event, all our efforts to capture the amazing experience on film were in vain. So what you can do, right now, is visit our Puerto Rico Resource Portal (http://bit.ly/PRportal) and click on the Bioluminescent Bay article to watch the professional video we found. And compared to the video, the real-life experience will blow you away.

The most popular Bio-Bay tours are Laguna Grande in Fajardo and Mosquito Bay in Vieques. Keep in mind that because they are unique and noteworthy, they may be crowded and thoroughly imitated by competing companies.

So, what is a "Bio Bay" and why should you tour one? Bio bays are rare natural phenomena where billions of bioluminescent aquatic microorganisms (plankton) concentrate near mangrove estuaries. When agitated, these tiny dinoflagellates produce a brief glow by the millions. The splash of an ore, a darting fish, or even the scoop of your hand into the water will produce the effect. Any sudden movement in the water is evidenced by an ethereal, ghostly blue glow. It's quite a sight!

Cost and Time

We had our own rental car and took the Bio-Bay tour via Pure Adventure tour in Fajardo, PR. Prices start at $48 per person (plus tax) and the tour lasts about two hours, which is a great deal because it's such a unique experience. Keep in mind any transit time from your home base in Puerto

Rico, e.g. from San Juan to Fajardo you should allow at least an hour to be on the safe side. Learn more at www.pureadventurepr.com.

There are usually two tours in Laguna Grande, one at around 5:30pm and one at about 7pm. You *must* be there early or they will leave without you so make sure to plan ahead if you are commuting in. We recommend the earlier tour because for two main reasons: 1) You'll have enough light to see the lovely mangroves, and 2) you get to enjoy sunset on the water!

What You Can Expect

- Arrive early and pay attention to the safety demonstration that the guide goes over, including details on safety gear and kayak maneuvering.
- Bring reef shoes and comfortable clothes you won't mind getting wet. You will need to get into the water for a bit before climbing into your kayak. And don't forget insect repellent!
- You will paddle out behind your guide through a narrow channel lined with majestic mangroves. Be prepared to use some upper body strength and do some maneuvering!
- You will all go out to the large bay and your guide will give you an overview of the bay, the plankton, and possibly even some constellations.
- As sun sets and the light fades, be prepared to be astonished to see the water begin to glow wherever there is motion – be it from your paddle, your hand, or even a fish zipping by underneath!
- You'll spend some time out in the bay just marveling at the experience, then as the later tour comes in you can begin paddling back.

A note about Bio Bays: you want to take into account the phase of the moon during your visit. The less moonlight you have, the better the experience. Also, because the plankton are dependent on such a delicate ecosystem, you definitely want to call ahead to ensure that conditions are right.

Because this is such a rare ecosystem and experience, we consider it a must-do activity. It's a natural wonder and the memory will stay with you for a lifetime.

Additional Guided Tours to the Bio-Bays

Viator's Kayak Bio Bay Tour in Fajardo: If you DO NOT have your own transportation, the Bio Bay experience is still available to you as this tour includes pick-up and drop-off from select San Juan hotels. This 4-hour tour features a professional guide and all orientations listed above. From $106 per person. Learn more at www.viator.com.

Viator's Bio-Bay Boat Tour to La Parguera: This is a great nighttime adventure departing from San Juan (w/convenient hotel pickup), and will be something of a sunset cruise. Your shuttle will drive you to the nearby coastal town of La Parguera, where you'll then enjoy the sunset from a boat which will then take you to the bioluminescent bay for additional marine wonders. When done you'll be driven back to your hotel. From $175 per person for about a 10-hour tour. Please note you'll be getting back to San Juan quite late. Learn more at www.viator.com.

Kayaking Puerto Rico Bio Bay Tour in Fajardo: This is the standard 2-hour Bio Bay guided kayak tour in Laguna Grande, and will offer transportation via shared ride IF there are 6 or more people needing the ride. You will need to check if they will pick you up. This would be a great option for a cruise group. Bio Bay tour starts at $48 per person and round-trip transport is $20 per person. 787-435-1665. Learn more at www.kayakingpuertorico.com.

13. SIX SAMPLE ITINERARIES

There is so much to do on this beautiful island and below are some ideas on how to arrange your vacation. Now, keep in mind these suggestions do not include travel days…if you arrive in the afternoon or leave in the morning you probably only have time to get settled or ready, have a nice meal and take care of travel logistics. So if you are arriving on Thursday night and leaving Sunday morning, you might look at the Two Days itinerary suggestion.

Secondly, this is a *vacation*, so it is perfectly fine to relax, sit on a beach and do nothing. The day plans below are merely suggestions to consider and incorporate at your own pace. Feel free to **mix and match** depending on your mood, preferences, and the weather.

One Day

This is perfect for cruise visitors, who usually have 9-10 hours to explore. Not to worry, Old San Juan has more than enough to keep someone busy for a day. You could easily explore Old San Juan for 2-3 days, so if you are really charmed by the atmosphere, architecture, history and shopping, you could definitely spend more time here.

Day 1 morning: Explore Cristobal Castle & El Morro

Day 1 afternoon/evening: Old San Juan walking tour & shopping

Two Days

Activities from One Day itinerary, adding: El Yunque and either Luquillo Beach OR Laguna Grande Bio Bay. If you do some forest hiking in the morning and want to relax, you can head to nearby Luquillo. If you feel up for kayaking, you will be close to the Fajardo Bio Bay and both of these activities together will give a day's worth of 100% Puerto Rico.

Day 2 morning: El Yunque National Forest

Day 2 afternoon/evening: Luquillo Beach OR Laguna Grande Bio Bay

Three Days

Activities of the prior days, adding: Arecibo and Rio Camuy Cave Park Day Trip or the Inner Loop Day Trip. Pack road snacks and leave early – either of these excursions will make for an action-packed day.

Day 3 morning: Arecibo Observatory and Rio Camuy Cave Park

Day 3 afternoon/evening: Finish tours, dinner in Arecibo, drive back.

--OR—

All Day Inner Loop Day Trip.

Four Days

Activities of the prior days, adding: Full Day Catamaran Snorkel Tour to Icacos. This is a laid-back tour which allows for relaxing on a boat, swimming, snorkeling, and seeing the unspoiled, uninhabited nearby island of Icacos.

Day 4 morning: Sail out, lunch on catamaran.

Day 4 afternoon/evening: Return sailing, get to home base in time for dinner.

Five Days

Activities of the prior days, adding: An off-island Day Trip to Vieques or Culebra. You may take the early ferry or fly out to either island, and select from the activities listed in Chapter 11.

Day 5 morning: Sail or fly out to Vieques or Culebra

Day 5 afternoon/evening: Find your favorite beach or participate in a guided tour. Catch ferry or plane back to Fajardo unless you are staying overnight.

Six Days or More

Activities of prior days, adding: Any option listed above that you haven't tried yet, any options from Chpater 10 OR revisiting something you've already done. For example, you may choose to go back to Old San Juan for more shopping and sightseeing, or back to El Yunque to hike a different set of trails.

You may also want to explore some of the more traditional activities that your hotel concierges are likely to recommend, such as parasailing or zip-lining. Almost any island will offer these options while Chapters 8 – 12 focus on activities that offer a more unique Puerto Rico experience.

If you are staying six days or more, congratulations! You are going to get a taste of the real Puerto Rico. If so far you have filled every single day with activity, chances are it might be time to just go sit on the beach and relax to the ocean's lullaby.

14. SUPPLIES – PUERTO RICO PACKING LIST

"Aw man, I really wish I had brought _____." Fill in the blank: insect repellent, a nail file, an umbrella, etc.

And now you're in a tourist area and have to pay possibly double for the item, or you'll have two of the same thing because you have "it" at home, or worst of all – you can't find what you need.

During our Puerto Rico vacation, we brought some things along that either saved our hides or made our trip that much better. And we forgot some others. We don't want you to have the same "oops" moments we did, so we've compiled a shopping list that will make your island getaway that much more enjoyable.

The benefit is that you'll also save money and time by not having to buy these things *while* on vacation. On the one hand, time you spend hunting for something trivial is cutting into your enjoyment time – and on the other, you will be paying the price of convenience. Hotels are happy to charge outrageous prices for items you may have forgotten. So please, before you leave, consider if you'd want to add any of the following items to your packing list...you probably have a few of these already at home.

The Essentials

Compact Travel Camera with HD Video. We took every single picture on this trip with the Nikon Coolpix P310 16.1MP 60x zoom and 1080p HD Video. Sadly, we discovered that Nikon is discontinuing most of its 300 series. If you can find one, this is a great point-and-shoot. But we wanted to offer another option so after lots of research, we finally landed on a good equivalent that's compact and has all the settings you could want for travel including 1080p HD video capability. It's the Canon PowerShot Elph (various models). Here's a link to them on Amazon: http://amzn.to/2dEUTpC

They are compact and stable, make sure the model you are looking at supports 1080p video. While this camera is affordably priced, there's one thing we recommend not skimping on and that's having a good travel camera.

Hydration Pack. Absolutely essential for beach time, hiking, touring Old San Juan and day trips. Ladies: consider not taking a purse – a hydro-pak is more convenient and won't leave you with a sore shoulder as you take long walks or hikes. Ideal travel hydro-packs are small to medium size and have secure compartments for: camera, binoculars, sunglasses, sunscreen, money/cards/ID/maps, and hiking snacks.

Important note: At least on Amazon, the price of hydration packs varies by color (presumably based on availability) – sometimes with a difference of $100 or more! The range is between $36 and a few over $100, so just keep an eye out.

Adventure Medical Kit – Travel Medic. We simply can't emphasize this enough -- every savvy traveler should have this kit. It provides the tremendous value of helping you feel better so you can enjoy your vacation, so it is worth its weight in gold. It's ultra compact and has all the remedies you need for blisters, headache, inflammation, allergies, and upset stomach. Trust us on this: you'd rather have it and not need it than need it and not have it!

3oz travel containers. Unless you're staying for more than a week, you can probably get away with just one piece of carry-on luggage. In that case, it's essential that you have TSA-compliant liquids containers. For Puerto Rico specifically you may want to pack: sunscreen, insect repellent, hair gel, aloe vera gel (in case of sunburn), and itch relief cream for insect bites. We like the GoToob brand. Here's a quick link to them: http://amzn.to/2dF5qfT

Rain Poncho. You could bring a compact umbrella, but a rain poncho with a hood is easier to roll up and pack, it will protect you better from sideways rain (if there is wind), and you can use it in a pinch as a picnic blanket or to make a clean spot to sit on if you're hiking.

Reef Shoes, aka "Aqua Socks." There are two big reasons to take water shoes, namely:

1. Most of the popular hotels have perfectly combed beaches with fine white sand. But if you decide to explore some of the other island beaches (we hope you do!) you will find coarser sand and rocky areas. We definitely encountered sharp but slippery rocks (from algae). Reef shoes will help protect your feet from sharp rocks or debris and give you better traction.

2. Puerto Rico has over 50 rivers, so if you are hiking in the mountains and rainforest, you will find lots of little creeks, some of which you may be interested in crossing. You will also find rocky waterfalls you may want to take a dip in. And because the mountains enjoy more rain, some of the trails will be muddy, which are no problem with washable water shoes.

Special Note for the Ladies, Regarding Makeup: don't bother packing anything other than lipstick and waterproof mascara – the humidity will melt anything else right off! There, now you have a little more packing space. :-)

The Little Extras

Eagle Creek Pack It Envelopes and Cubes. Aside from the genius idea of adding wheels to luggage (it only took thousands of years for humans to think this up) – the "Pack-It" line can significantly change the way you travel. These envelopes, cubes and sleeves look deceptively simple but their compression keeps your clothes neat, wrinkle-free and efficiently compressed is a travel game-changer. This system is a lot more effective than stuffing your clothes down, or even rolling them.

The size "18" envelope is perfect for your island getaway carry-on bag since you can easily fold five days' worth of hiking, leisure and beach clothes because the Velcro strips allow you compress your things down into an ultra-compact envelope. The line features various colors, just beware you may form a slight dependency on them.

Here is a short link to Eagle Creek listings on Amazon:
http://amzn.to/2dqAgtE

Mini Travel bluetooth speaker. In case you would like to listen to your portable music device in your room, on the beach, in the rainforest, or really anywhere – there are a variety of portable speakers with a big sound…they even have waterproof options! You can enjoy your playlist anywhere with this little device that fits in the palm of your hand.

Here is a short link to mini Bluetooth speakers on Amazon: https://amzn.to/2WIzGko

Travel Binoculars. This is one of the items we really wish we had brought. From the beach, you can spot cruise liners coming in in the distance. Many of the historic spots offer elevated vistas where you are treated to breathtaking panoramas of the city and ocean. And from the mountains, the views are…otherworldly. Especially high up in the rainforest, we wished we'd had a pair of binoculars to see if we could spot any of the island birds whenever we'd hear a rustling. A small pair shouldn't add too much weight and will offer you the option to see things from a different perspective.

Duolingo Online Language Training (FREE). Nervous because you've forgotten your semester of high school Spanish? Through the magic of technology and some really smart developers, Duolingo is a fantastic new free language course that you can use on both your desktop, laptop, and even mobile device. Here are our three tips to get you conversational before you head out:

1. Sign up for Duolingo and download their app to your mobile device. Using an intuitive interface and a reward system that makes learning feel like a game, this free service is a winner. For the full low-down you can read the review on our website by clicking here: http://bit.ly/DLingo
2. Consider creating a Spanish music playlist and changing your entertainment viewing to be in Spanish (with English subtitles). You can either rent Spanish movies for your local video store or add new movies to your online streaming service. This level of immersion will help you gain a much better grasp of the language, but you must do it diligently.
3. We've written an article on our site that goes into more detail on how to do a crash course. It's called "Foreign Language for Travel: How to Learn Quickly" and here is a short link: http://bit.ly/Lang4Trav

During your Trip: Souvenirs

While you can find souvenirs close to any of the tourist hotels, here are a few thoughts on purchasing souvenirs:

- The further away you are from the tourist areas, the less expensive souvenirs will be. Consider looking in another city or municipality if you take a day trip.
- Consider how easy the souvenir(s) will be to pack, e.g. size, weight, fragility.
- Consider supporting the Puerto Rico economy by buying local artisan items versus printed items -- which may have been made in a foreign country. We found an impressive selection of unique local jewelry, painting, photography and sculpture – you wouldn't believe the beautiful masks that can be made from coconut husks!
- Puerto Rico souvenirs are not as abundant online as they are on the island, so make sure you get anything you'd like while you're there to play it safe.

15. TOP FOUR LESSONS WE LEARNED

First, we should just get it out there that the biggest, most obvious thing we learned is that Puerto Rico is a fascinating island with lots to offer. This is why we decided to document and share our experience – to demonstrate that a really fulfilling vacation can be accomplished on modest means. Our hope is that by implementing this approach, you can discover it for yourself.

Research pays off! By investing time and energy up front, you can find better deals, discounts, reduced rates, and have a better range of options to compare. This applies to your big-ticket vacation expenses: airfare, lodging, and car rental.

Balance planning and spontaneity. With regards to activities during your stay, we recommend having some items planned, but not being attached to a rigorous itinerary. For two reasons:

You want to be flexible enough that you can respond to the weather. For example, if you're met with a rainy day, that's probably best for a day trip where you can stay dry in the car.

Allow extra time for your activities so that you can feel free to explore – going off on side streets to check out little shops, or stopping at a beachfront restaurant. These unplanned detours may lead to some of your best holiday memories.

Be mindful of "tourist traps." We're not suggesting that you avoid touristy areas – after all, people gravitate toward beauty (whether it's historic or natural) and you want to see that. Just be aware that:

- The tourist industry charges a premium for goods, services, and activities.

- Heavily "Americanized" areas or experiences aren't giving you the best taste of Puerto Rican culture.

Be prepared to step outside your comfort zone. Although Puerto Rico has been a U.S. territory for over a hundred years, it does not feel like the U.S. mainland – that's part of its charm! Consider that English is not the primary language, the island-wide economy has had some challenges, and there are cultural differences. Oh yes, and the driving (see Chapter 5). But if you're willing to take on some of the unfamiliar, you will absolutely reap the rewards of getting to know this beautiful island and its friendly people.

ABOUT THE AUTHORS

We love sharing travel hacks and encouraging others to make time for exploration, for vacation, and for reconnecting with themselves.

Favorite Puerto Rico Memories:

"I have to say it was night-kayaking in the bioluminescent bay, scooping up handfuls of water and watching all these microscopic plankton light up in my hands like glowing glitter. Unforgettable."

"Hands down, driving through the misty mountains. With all its twists and turns and dense foliage, it was an otherworldly experience."

You are cordially invited to visit our website:
http://www.happyholidaysguides.com

Made in United States
Orlando, FL
07 December 2022

25672636R00050